Mel Robinson is a writer, mother, and unintentional expert in emotional logistics. She writes for midlife women carrying invisible wounds and unspoken grief — those still bandaging the past while trying to remember the version of themselves that once dared to dream. Drawing from real-life experiences, she writes with humour and heart about the chaos, grief, and unexpected grace of midlife. This is her debut book.

THIS WASN'T THE PLAN

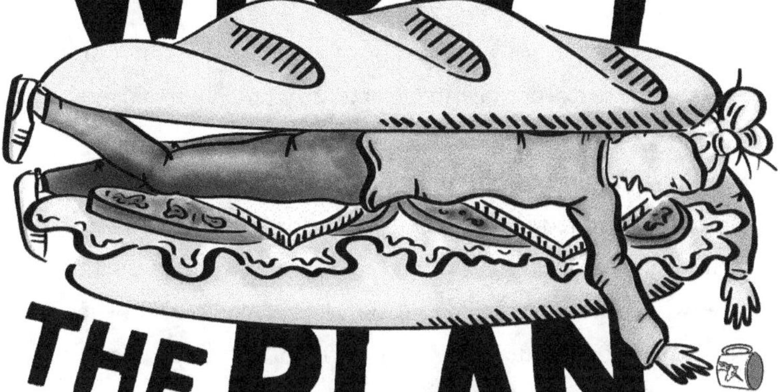

Grieving the Golden Years That Never Came

MEL ROBINSON

ALKIRA
PUBLISHING

This Wasn't the Plan: Grieving the Golden Years That Never Came
Mel Robinson
Copyright © 2025
Published by Alkira Publishing
ABN: 32736122056
http://www.alkirapublishing.com

All characters in this publication are fictitious and any resemblance to real persons, living or dead, is purely coincidental.

All rights reserved. No part of this publication may be reproduced, stored in a retrieval system or transmitted in any form or by any means electronic, mechanical, audio, visual or otherwise, without prior permission of the copyright owner. Nor can it be circulated in any form of binding or cover other than that in which it is published and without similar conditions including this condition being imposed on the subsequent purchaser.

ISBN: 978-1-922329-91-2

Illustrations by Hayley Langsdorf
https://thoughtsdrawnout.com.au/

Dedicated to:
Peace and Quiet
Always and Forever, Mum

CHAPTER 1:
Retirement? I Hardly Know Her.

NARRATIVE

Just when I started pricing flights and picturing solitude, my grown kids came home—with duffel bags and dreams of staying rent free.

Retirement wasn't cancelled. It just got rescheduled … indefinitely.

It turns out the golden years might be gilded in dog hair and empty Gatorade bottles.

You grow up thinking there are chapters to life. Childhood. Uni or work. Marriage. Maybe kids. And then—if you do all the right things and don't completely stuff it up—comes the bit where you

This Wasn't the Plam

finally get to live your life.

My parents certainly believed in that timeline. By the time I finished high school, they were already planning 'the big trip'. Europe. Maybe Alaska. A reward, apparently—for successfully raising a child who didn't get expelled and could string a sentence together. A thank-you tour for making it through eighteen years without setting the kitchen on fire or forgetting to pick me up from school (too often). They packed their suitcases, kissed me goodbye, and essentially said, 'Right. That's our job done.'

There were no ongoing emotional check-ins. No talk of university fees, or helping me find a new rental place, or gently explaining how to vote. Just a quiet, comfortable confidence that I'd figure it out. Their reward for parenting? Freedom. And maybe some duty-free gin.

So naturally, when my own kids hit their final year of school, I assumed I was approaching my big exhale. One was out. One was nearly done. There were flickers of light at the end of the tunnel— the kind you see when you've been shovelling out school lunches and paying off school fees since the Spice Girls were together.

I imagined retirement in a dreamy kind of way—not in a 'golf and garden centre' way, but in a me-time way. A 'long-lunching, wine-tasting, booking-flights-without-checking-school-holidays' kind of way. The version of adulthood where you actually get to nap and nobody needs to know where the cordless vacuum is.

For a while, I really believed it. I'd done my time. I'd launched them into the world. Cue freedom.

Only ... they came back. Or rather, they never fully left.

'It's too expensive to rent while I'm trying to save.'

'Do you know how much a loaf of bread is?'

'The job market is a flaming bin fire of "entry level" roles that demand five years' experience and a diploma in wizardry.'

So, digging in their heels, they came—dragging laundry baskets, emotional baggage, and assumptions that the fridge magically refills itself.

And just when I was calculating how many unused school-fee payments I could funnel into a cheeky solo trip to Spain, I realised something devastating: **My nest wasn't empty. It was just in renovation.**

This Wasn't the Plam

THREADED PARENTAL LAYER

To be fair, I never quite had the place to myself.

My parents—Mum and Dad—have lived in the granny flat on our property since the kids were little. We built it when we bought the house. "Granma's Cubby", we called it. It was meant to be a win-win: support and company for them, a bit of help with the kids for us, and the bonus of always having someone nearby to water the plants when we were away. (Not that we were away often—sigh.)

Everyone got on well for the most part. Mum loved being involved—dropping by with a cup of tea and a hot take on current affairs whether you wanted one or not. Dad managed the finances with military precision. Their presence was lovely ... mostly. Occasionally stifling. Like when you're trying to sneak a gin and tonic at 3:30 pm on a Wednesday and your father wanders through asking if you know what 'Bitcoin' is.

Back then, I used to fantasise about an empty house. Just me. No kids. No impromptu chats about climate policy or the latest 'colossal waste of electricity'.

Just ... peace.

Turns out, peace is still pending.

This Wasn't the Plan

MINI SCENE: WHO EVEN LEAVES THE NEST ANYMORE?

Living Room. Friday Afternoon

Mum is on the couch, scrolling through travel blogs on her iPad.

Adult Child #1 (yelling from bedroom): 'Muuuuum! We outta juice?'

Mum: 'You mean, are we out of juice?'

Adult Child #1: 'Whatever. Just checking.'

Mum: 'Check with your eyes, not your mouth. And if we are, the shops are exactly two streets away.'

Adult Child #1 (sincerely confused): 'So … like … you want me to go?'

Insert quiet screaming into a decorative throw pillow.

Mel Robinson

FAKE SOCIAL POST

Instagram Caption:

Thought I was entering the golden years of long lunches, unlimited travel and silence.
Instead, I'm still making lunches, dreaming of travel, and being asked where the peanut butter lives by a fully grown human with stink lines.
#EmptyNestMyArse #RetirementRescheduled #ParentsTheATM

REFLECTION

They don't tell you this part.

They tell you parenting ends when high school does. That your kids will fly the coop. That your reward for years of unpaid emotional labour is independence—and maybe a quiet lounge room.

But sometimes the nest stays full. Or it empties and refills.

Or it never quite clears, because other people—your own parents—are still nearby, still needing you in a hundred small ways. And suddenly, the freedom you were promised feels like a story someone else got to live.

And you?

This Wasn't the Plan

You're still here.
Making dinner.
Running group chats.
Wondering when it's going to be your turn.

CHAPTER 2:
When Everyone Around You Grows Up, But You're Still Tired

THE BIRTH OF THE PEACE ROOM

When we bought the house, the real estate agent used the classic catchphrase—'a fixer-upper with potential'. Sitting on the toilet, you could literally see the dirt floor through the holes in the boards. So yes, potential. But also: tetanus.

It was a massive undertaking, especially while raising small children. Renovating around toddlers is a bit like trying to perform open-heart surgery on a rollercoaster. Slowly, we chipped away at it. And

This Wasn't the Plam

eventually, we finished what the kids called 'the big room'. Half became a formal dining space, and the other half ... well, I wasn't sure what to do with it.

We're not 'formal lounge' people. When we entertain, it's a BBQ out the back with music, wine, and the kind of laughter that gets louder the later it gets. The thought of creating a room just to sit quietly and behave felt foreign. But then it clicked—maybe this wasn't for guests. Maybe it could be ... for me.

I bought candles. Crystals. A soft couch. A reading lamp. A coffee table that served no real purpose other than making the room look intentional. I didn't even know what to call it at first. But then the kids started asking, 'Where's Mum?' and the answer became automatic:

'Shh. She's in the Peace Room.'

The name stuck.

EARLY DAYS OF CALM

The first few visits felt a bit ... sneaky. Like I was shirking responsibility. Should I be batch-cooking lasagnas instead of sitting cross-legged on the couch, flipping through a novel I'd already started twice before? Probably. But also ... no.

This was my rebellion. A space in the house that wasn't about feeding, cleaning, sorting, solving, reminding. A space that smelled like vanilla and self-respect.

And for a little while, it worked.

THE GREAT PEACE ROOM HEIST

It started with a quiet *poof*—the sound of a fully grown adult flopping onto my sacred throw cushions like they were calling dibs on my peace.

'Mum? Can I ask you something?'

At first, it seemed innocent.

Tiny jobs. Minor missions.

Friend drama. Course confusion. Existential spirals about future careers.

It felt like bonding, not burglary.

I thought I was offering a pop-in advice booth. Five minutes in, five minutes out.

Low commitment. High wisdom.

This Wasn't the Plam

And then the heist began.
One kid turned into two.
Two turned into two plus the boyfriend.
Next thing I knew, I was hosting nightly emotional crisis meetings without pay or snacks.
Job rejection meltdowns.
Flatmate betrayal debriefs.
Midnight Medicare tutorials.
HECS debt existential dread at sunrise.
My Peace Room—once the Zen temple where I lit candles and breathed like a well-adjusted adult—had been *quietly overtaken*.

COMING SOON TO A NETFLIX DOCUMENTARY NEAR YOU:

The Great Peace Room Heist:
One Woman.
Zero Boundaries.
No One Asked Permission.
Starring me in the combined role of therapist, unpaid intern, and occasional hostage.

EMOTIONAL LABOUR 2.0

The Peace Room became the Holding Room. Not just for their emotions, but mine too.

Because when your daughter crumples onto your couch, saying she doesn't know what to do with her life, you don't respond with, 'Well, I was actually just halfway through a guided meditation.'

You listen.

You soothe.

You summon your last reserves of empathy even though you gave most of them to a tax form at 10 am.

And then you sit there alone afterward, in the candlelight, wondering when someone might ask *you* how you're doing.

ZINGERS AND PASSIVE-AGGRESSIVE ENLIGHTENMENT

Occasionally, sarcasm would sneak in.

'Ohh sweetie, you have such a hard life—living in this tiny home, paying no rent, and having your every need met.'

'This isn't a drop-in centre. It's not even a therapy room. It was meant to be a Peace Room. Peace. You remember peace?'

They'd laugh. Sort of.
So would I. Sort of.

WHAT IT SAYS ABOUT MOTHERHOOD

I think back to my own mum. Around birthdays, I'd always ask her what she wanted. When I was little, she'd say, 'A mink coat', which made no sense because we lived in a subtropical climate.

As I got older, her wish changed: 'Peace and quiet.'

At the time, I thought that was a boring answer. We had plenty of quiet. What I didn't realise was she wasn't asking for silence—she was asking for space. Autonomy. Release from the constant emotional thread-pulling that is motherhood.

She wanted a Peace Room.

She never got one.

I built one—and I still don't get to use it.

REFLECTION

You can carve out corners of your home, but carving out corners of your life? That's harder.

You tell yourself:

This is survivable. It's temporary. Just a few more months.

This Wasn't the Plam

But months turn into years. And suddenly, the 'phase' you were tolerating becomes your new normal.

The irony is that the Peace Room—meant to be my sanctuary—became the proof that I was still doing the job I thought I'd retired from.

Mothering doesn't end. It just relocates.

Sometimes ... to the room with the nice candles.

CHAPTER 3
The Travel That Never Was

TRAVEL FANTASIES

Everyone has a bucket list.

For some, it's sipping wine in Tuscany. For others, it's dangling off a rope on Kilimanjaro.

Me?

Mine was practical, but it still had a sparkle:

The Northern Lights.

The Amazon.

Standing under Christ the Redeemer in Rio, arms wide like, *'Look at me, Mum—no hands, no helmets, I'm still standing.'*

But here's the thing they don't put on travel brochures: You need a life with gaps big enough to step through.

This Wasn't the Plam

And ours?

Tighter than a carry-on after a midlife crisis shopping spree.

With a schoolteacher husband and kids who scheduled their minor meltdowns like clockwork, our travel windows were laughable.

Two weeks in April.

Two in September.

Never quite enough to justify hauling ourselves from Australia to anywhere that felt like a dream.

So I cut a deal with the future.

Later, I promised myself.

Later, we'll slip onto last-minute flights and sip midday wines without anyone asking for emergency dental forms or a lift to soccer.

I pictured it vividly:

Après-ski in Europe.

Mink coat thrown over my shoulders. (Fake fur, obviously. I'm loyal to my mother's glamour but not ready to get cancelled by Gen Z.)

Maybe even a small, slightly ridiculous hat I couldn't explain but wore anyway.

But the truth is, it wasn't about ticking off destinations.

It was about escaping the gravitational pull of being needed.

I didn't imagine strolling into a café with glossy

hair and a fake laugh.

I imagined sitting at a table alone, unbothered, coat slipping off one shoulder, drinking a glass of something cold, and nobody needing a damn thing from me.

No questions.
No errands.
No 'Mum, can you just …'
Just me.
Taking up space like I meant it.

POP CULTURE PIPE DREAMS

Long before I understood the concept of 'me time', I watched *Fantasy Island*. Guests arrived in private planes. Their deepest wishes were granted without them having to explain themselves. It wasn't the location I loved—it was the ease.

No one asked if you were sure you locked the back door.

No one needed an ATM transfer.

You didn't have to *schedule your joy.*

As a child, I didn't know what I was really seeing. But now? Oh, I see it.

I wasn't dreaming of a destination.

I was dreaming of being *seen*, supported, and uninterrupted.

COMPARISONS: THE 'LUCKY' ONES

Some parents I knew had already cashed in. Holidays in Europe. Girls' trips to Bali. Couples' weekends with actual sleeping in. They'd sigh dramatically about flying business instead of first class, and I'd try to nod sympathetically, even as I eyed the grocery bill and counted how many school-fee payments we *could have* spent on a beachside suite in Noosa.

Then there were the divorced mums. *They* had it sorted. One week on, one week off. Every second weekend free to run away to a winery and find themselves again. It almost looked appealing … until I remembered the 'on' weeks came back. With full force. Alone.

Still, for a while, the fantasy held.

LOST OPPORTUNITIES

Working for myself had a lot of perks. Flexibility. Autonomy. Pyjamas as workwear.

But it also meant that I could scale back easily when family needs rose up—and they always rose up. I'd reduce my hours to be the taxi, the nurse, the shoulder, the admin officer, the lunch-box stockist. And it worked.

Until it didn't.

Because when the kids saw me working part time, they didn't see *work*. They saw *availability*.

'You're not working tomorrow, right? Can you take me to Bunnings? I need cardboard for a uni assignment.'

'Do we have any almond flour? I'm baking for work again.'

'Can you help me with my CV? This job closes in thirty minutes.'

I had dreams of starting pottery. A writing course. Even an interior styling class. But those were always *someday* things.

And *someday*, I realised, had started passing me by.

THE QUIET GRIEF

Here's the thing: parenting doesn't end. And for a lot of us, freedom never starts.

You don't get a certificate. Or a party. You don't wake up one day and find your schedule is yours again. Instead, you wake up to questions. Noise. Texts. Requests. Groceries gone missing. And that ever-lingering whisper in your head:

I thought this part would be different.

I didn't want to whinge. My kids are kind. Funny.

This Wasn't the Plam

Capable. They're becoming wonderful adults.

But when they were younger, I was raised on the narrative that your kids leave home and that's when *you* begin.

It's not about a villa in Tuscany. It's not about Instagram sunsets or fresh croissants in Paris.

It's about feeling like your life is yours again.

And when that doesn't happen? You grieve. Quietly. While you're cleaning up the baking mess from muffins you didn't even get to eat.

REFLECTION

There's a grief no one warns you about: the grief of a life you planned, but never lived.

You don't resent the people who held you back. But you start to notice all the little things you lost along the way.

Freedom.

Time.

Spontaneity.

Choice.

And you wonder if one day, when it's finally 'your turn', you'll even know what to do with it.

CHAPTER 4:
The Financial Drip Feed (a.k.a. How We Accidentally Became an ATM)

FUNDING THE FREELOADERS (WITH LOVE)

There are the big-ticket items you brace yourself for—education, second-hand cars, the occasional dental apocalypse. And then there's the drip feed.

The endless, soul-chipping trickle of minor expenses that sneaks into your bank account like gremlins at midnight:
- Netflix
- Stan

This Wasn't the Plam

- Spotify
- Phone plans
- Gym memberships
- Orthotics
- Protein powder (WHY is it priced like it's made from unicorns?)
- Dentists
- Doctors
- Health insurance (at that price, they *better* cover emotional injuries)
- Uni textbooks
- Wi-Fi
- And the casual, 'While you're at the shops, can you grab deodorant, soy milk and those muesli bars I like? Thanks, love you!'

(*Translation: No, you will not be reimbursed. Yes, you are expected to smile anyway.*)

And just when you adjust to the slow bleed, the ambush hits:

- 'Oh BTW, I joined rugby. It's $300 for the season. Plus gear. Also … I'm at the hospital. Minor jaw surgery. No big deal.'
- 'Don't touch anything in the freezer. It's all for camping.'

(*Translation: Your sausages, burger patties, foil, matches and patience have been commandeered for a gourmet bush adventure.*)

Mel Robinson

At some point—and there wasn't an announcement, a warning, or even a half-hearted thank you—we realised something:

We weren't just raising adults.

We were running an unlicensed bank, a crisis hotline, and a gourmet grocery delivery service.

And business?

Booming.

#ApplicationsForRefundsAreCurrently
ClosedIndefinitely

This Wasn't the Plam

GROCERY GAUNTLET

The weekly shop used to last a week. Then the adult children moved in.

Suddenly, I was shopping every three days, and the food vanished faster than it entered the fridge. I started hiding the 'good snacks'. I labelled things. I developed mild paranoia around missing chocolate.

To make matters worse, my eldest became the *office baker*. Which sounds sweet. Until you realise, she used *my* pantry to supply her team with flourless chocolate cake and themed cupcakes. Not only did I get none of the goods—**I cleaned up the war zone she left behind.**

And when I reached for the vanilla extract or caster sugar?

'Oh, we're out. Sorry. I used the last of it for Sarah's birthday muffins.'

Sarah doesn't live here, sweetie.

LIVING COST LOGIC
(AND THE MYTH OF 'RENT')

At some point, I did try to draw the line.

We asked her to contribute a little rent.

Cue the shock. The gasps. The whispered betrayal.

'But I'm saving for a house!'
'You want me to pay to live at HOME?'
'I'm your CHILD!'

We settled on a modest amount. Think: a symbolic gesture toward adulthood. Barely enough to cover two days of Wi-Fi and the electricity to run the Nutri Bullet.

Even then, I had to *remind her* when it was due.

Eventually, she agreed to set up an automatic transfer. I celebrated like I'd won Lotto—Division 6, but still.

Of course, the logic then evolved:

'Since I'm paying rent ... does that include shampoo? And oat milk? And a new pair of sneakers? And can I borrow your credit card for a sec?'

My credit card became the magic wand. It was used for:

'Emergency party drinks'

'Just grabbing sushi'

'A birthday gift for someone you don't even know'

I tried to keep a straight face, but my internal monologue was screaming:

Sweetheart, rent does not include a lifestyle subscription. I am not Afterpay. Or Uber Eats. I am a woman on the edge.

EMOTIONAL TANGLE

There's a constant tug-of-war between pride and resentment.

I love that they're saving. I love that they're smart. I love that they trust me.

But I also want to scream into the void:

Why is it still me?

Why is my money still the fallback plan?

Why does no one seem to realise I didn't get to stay at home and pay nothing and build a stockpile of cash?

One child did move out for a while. Share house. Five boys. No photos were ever shared. I admired the independence but still found myself topping up petrol and sending food home like I was on a care package rotation for a war zone.

It wasn't the money. It was the mental load of always being the backup.

ZINGERS I HAVE SAID (AND MEANT)

- 'Do you know how much that costs?'
- 'Rent does NOT include your lifestyle.'
- 'If it's empty, you can walk to the shops.'
- 'I'm not the only one who knows how to go to Coles.'

- 'The credit card is for emergencies. Taking a carton of beer to a party is NOT an emergency.'

But mostly, I kept it together. I muttered under my breath. I let them live their lives. Paid for the almond butter ... again.

REFLECTION

This chapter isn't just about money.

It's about invisible labour.

About how the *support* you offer—financial, emotional, practical—starts out temporary, and then ... never ends.

You love them. You'd do anything for them.

But somewhere along the way, you start whispering to yourself:

This was supposed to be my turn.

And every time they swipe your card—or just forget to say thanks—you feel the weight of that unfinished sentence growing heavier.

CHAPTER 5:
When the Kids Don't Launch (But You're the One in Orbit)

THE BLIP THAT WOULDN'T END

There's this quiet myth that hums under the breath of every sleep-deprived parent. A promise. A whisper. A fantasy dressed in sensible shoes:

Once the kids are done with school, you get your life back.

Cue the triumphant movie montage: sipping hot coffee, reclaiming your weekends, discovering hobbies that don't involve yelling reminders or decoding school emails.

Except … the credits didn't roll. There was no fade to black. No gentle violin music to carry me into a phase of rest and reinvention.

What happened instead felt less like a second act and more like a reboot I didn't agree to.

The exact moment I knew this 'blip' wasn't ending was graduation number two. The youngest tossed his cap in the air, and I swear, my nervous system lit up like it had just finished a marathon— *We made it! It's over! Breathe!*

And then he said, with the breezy delusion only a 17-year-old can manage:

'I'm going into law … and I might as well tack on a second degree.'

That sentence should come with an emotional health warning.

There it was: my phantom finish line, vanishing like a mirage.

The 'almost there' I'd been clutching like a rosary bead disintegrated in one moment of ambition I was supposed to be proud of. And I was proud. I was also … not okay.

I wasn't free. I was just shifting roles in the same dysfunctional theatre troupe.

By now, I had accumulated a gold medal in reheating coffee. I could run Medicare consults with my parents while refereeing soy milk debates between my kids. My mornings sounded less like a meditative ritual and more like:

'Dad, no, you can't apply for the pension online. Yes, I know it says, "Click here". No, not that click. That's a scam. STOP CLICKING.'

If my life had a subtitle, it would be: 'Living in a share house we pay the mortgage for.'

This is not the sequel I had in mind.

I thought midlife would look like reclaimed peace.

Instead, it's mostly me making silent eye contact with the kettle at 3 pm., wondering if I should just drink the damn tea cold or keep pretending I'll get to it.

I keep hearing people say, 'It's just a blip.'

Sweetheart—blips don't last this long.

This isn't a blip. This is the plot.

And somehow, I'm still in it.

THE NOT-SO-EMPTY NEST

Our house isn't small. The kids have their own rooms. They share a bathroom. We even set up a shared home office because we had a no-computers-in-bedrooms policy—based on the solid belief that the internet is a jungle, and no one needs to be watching YouTube documentaries on serial killers at 2 am in their pyjamas.

I thought the space would save us. What I hadn't counted on was becoming the hostess of the unofficial pre-drinks HQ for half the city.

See, being close to the city centre and the seedy nightclubs (sorry, cool bars for youths), our home became the gathering place for 'pre's'. For the blissfully unaware, 'pre's' are when your adult children and their friends drink your booze on your back veranda before going out to drink even more expensive booze elsewhere. The logic is simple: get tipsy at home, spend less out. Budgeting 101, apparently.

The budget-minded part of me almost respected the strategy. The cranky, sleep-deprived part of me did not.

Friday nights turned into episodes of *Survivor: Home Edition*, with me trying to pretend I didn't hear drunken laughter echoing down the hallway while I lay in bed Googling 'cheap off-grid cabins with no Wi-Fi.'

Eventually, after a few firm boundaries were set (and one incident involving glitter, a broken glass, and a badly timed vomit), the house was mostly retired as a launchpad for chaos. But the message had been received loud and clear: this was not the freedom I'd been promised.

This Wasn't the Plam

THE JOB APPLICATIONS THAT WEREN'T MINE, BUT FELT LIKE THEY WERE

It always started with a sigh. A half-hearted request. A vague, defeated:

'Mum, can you just help me write it? I don't know where to start.'

Of course they didn't. That was the point.

I'd done it professionally for years. Clients paid for this exact service—CV makeovers, cover letters that didn't sound like they were written by ChatGPT with a hangover, interview coaching that turned fear into confidence. It was my sweet spot.

But this wasn't a client. This was my child.

And there's something about coaching your own child that comes with a special kind of pain—an ache in the soul that says:

You know this will drain you, but you'll do it anyway.

I didn't get eye contact. Or follow-through. Or thank-yous.

I got the back end of their burnout. The sighs. The eye rolls. The disappearing act when it came time to revise the résumé I'd just spent hours on. I was fighting their resistance with my hope.

It felt like trying to start a fire in the rain.

But I couldn't abandon them. Even as it

chipped away at me. Even as my professional clarity dissolved into maternal doubt. I stayed. I rewrote. I followed up. I reminded. I coached.

Because if they didn't get the job, it wouldn't just be a missed opportunity. It would be a confirmation of their worst fear—and mine—that maybe they just weren't good enough.

So I held the line. Again.

And I told myself:

They'll understand one day.

I didn't know if that was true, but I needed to believe it anyway.

MINI SCENE: THE STEALTH BOYFRIEND

Kitchen. Saturday morning.

Mum opens the fridge. Notices the cooked chicken has diminished to a solitary drumstick.

Mum: 'We're going through food like an army on a mission.'

Daughter (casual): 'Oh, probably just him getting a snack.'

Mum: 'Him?' (also thinking a whole chicken can't be a 'snack')

Daughter: 'Yeah ... you know ... he's just been staying here a bit more lately. It's easier for work.

This Wasn't the Plam

Less time on the train.'

Cue internal alarm bells.

What started as the occasional overnight visit with the polite, easy-going boyfriend had quietly evolved into something closer to a full-time housemate.

Another pair of sneakers kicked off at the door. Another half-empty coffee mug appearing on the kitchen counter. Another Netflix account logged in and ready to go.

They weren't breeding, thank God, but the energy in the house was shifting—stretching to accommodate one more person without anyone officially announcing it.

I wasn't mad. Honestly, he was lovely

But lovely doesn't do the dishes.

The house, my routines, even my hard-won glimpses of freedom—they were quietly, almost sweetly, being swallowed up again.

This wasn't the plan. It was the slow, quiet replacement of the life I thought I'd be living.

Mel Robinson

SOCIAL POST

Facebook Status:

Thought I was done raising humans.
Turns out I'm now running a community centre.
Two kids. One boyfriend. HECS debts greater than our national GDP. All funded by the Parents' Magical Money Tree™.
#AreYourArmsPaintedOn #MyFridgeIsNotACharity #EmptyNestDelusion

MONEY, HONEY

We had a rule: learning or earning. That meant no 'gap year' on the couch, watching Netflix and becoming an expert in serial killer documentaries. I thought that covered everything.

What I failed to consider was who would be paying for the learning.

Yes, they work part time. No, that can't cover everything. And I get it—uni is full-on. But somehow, my grocery bills went up, the Spotify account has more users than people in the house, and my almond butter keeps disappearing during 'camping trips with the gang'.

Honestly, I'm not even mad about the study. I'm just confused about when I agreed to fund a Netflix-enabled hostel that smells faintly of Lynx and regret.

Mel Robinson

LEGACY VS REALITY

A friend told me once how, after she finished school, her parents helped her move to the city, gave her a little rent support, then promptly bought a caravan and vanished into the outback. There was no check-in. No 'How are your classes going?' No financial follow-up. Just … gone.

She laughed about it at the time.

But I sat there thinking—wait, that wasn't just me?

Turns out, our parents raised us, clapped politely when we graduated, and left us to it. Parenting was complete. Fin. Caput.

So what the hell happened?

Did we miss a memo? Was there a secret parenting handbook they forgot to give us at the hospital? Were we too emotionally available? Did we accidentally sign up for the deluxe package with lifetime support?

I don't know. But I do know this:

My son drinks a lot of smoothies, and I'm the one paying for the protein powder.

This Wasn't the Plan

REFLECTION

The hardest part isn't the extra laundry or the late-night door slams or the mysteriously disappearing groceries.

It's that you realise you're still orbiting around them—emotionally, financially, logistically—while they float in and out, trying to figure out how to adult.

You don't resent them. Not really. But you do grieve the life you thought would start when they graduated.

Because it hasn't.

Not yet.

And you're still waiting for launch.

CHAPTER 6:
No One Told Me There'd Be No Finish Line

SHIFTING GEARS

I was beginning to think that maybe—yes, *maybe*—there was a glimmer of hope on the horizon.

The youngest was happily share-housing, working part time, and smashing it at uni (mother of the year goes to me!!). The eldest was still living at home (sigh) with the boyfriend (double sigh), but at least she was contributing to the costs of running the house, making a few meals, and generally blending into our environment like a surprisingly efficient housemate.

Granpa and Granma had settled into their

own little ecosystem of medical appointments, book clubs, and low-stakes pensioner shenanigans. Things didn't *feel* easy, but they also didn't feel like a bushfire emergency every second Tuesday.

I even started Googling holidays. Where to next?

Hiking Machu Picchu had always tugged at my soul. Maybe a few weeks (yes, you heard me right— *weeks!*) leaving our lives in the hands of a guide, no thinking, no meal prep. Just us, backpacks, and a playlist of emotional support music.

Look at me! A woman on the brink of freedom. Not a breakdown.

RECLAIMING SPACE (OR NOT)

Like any middle-aged woman gasping for air between obligations, I tried to 'reset' my life.

I love a good retreat. Bonus points if it involves saltwater, journaling prompts, and someone else making lunch. The kids call them my 'hippy camps'. I call them medically necessary exits.

And the time away is magical. But the prep? Olympic level.

Frozen meals. Clean sheets. Pantry restocked. Passive-aggressive fridge notes like

PLEASE EAT ME. I'M ALREADY COOKED.'

And then I return to a house that looks like a crime scene staged by teenagers and wolves. Laundry. Chaos. Tattle-tales. The scent of passive neglect wafting through the kitchen.

Was it worth it?

Yes.

Was it restful?

Absolutely not.

THE MIRROR MOMENT

We were in the Peace Room—the soft chair, the salt lamp, that weird tissue box cover she made in Grade 4 that somehow never left. It was the same room where so many invisible breakdowns had happened. Mostly mine.

She was slouched in the corner chair, laptop open, jaw tight. That familiar tone in her voice—frustrated, tired, done.

'I've written the application. I've even found the jobs. But he just … won't do it. It's like pulling teeth. I'm doing everything I can to help, and it's still not enough.'

I didn't say anything. I just watched her. Watched her wrestle with that invisible weight I'd carried for years.

And then it happened. She looked up.

'Wow,' she said, blinking slowly. 'I'm honestly in awe of how you helped me all those years—even when I wasn't helping myself. I never knew how exhausting it was.'

Just like that, the loop closed.

She didn't know how exhausting it was.

Until she did.

And in her voice, I heard the thing I hadn't even realised I'd been waiting for:

Acknowledgment.

Not applause. Not some grand apology. Just recognition.

No invoice. No spotlight.

Just love, wrapped in effort.

And, finally, seen.

Right there, in the Peace Room. The site of so many battles.

This time, there was no fight.

Just a quiet kind of grace.

WHEN THEY START PARENTING YOU (... SORT OF)

Sometimes they say things like, 'Mum, don't cook tonight—we'll order something.' Or 'Don't worry, I'll put the laundry on.'

Cue a tiny hope blossom in my chest ... which

promptly shrivels the next morning when I find the washing machine full of damp clothes that now smell like despair and mildew.

And look, I know I *sound* ungrateful, but surely, I'm not the only one?

They mean well. But execution? Not their strong suit.

The intention is sweet. The aftermath is feral

It's like being offered a foot rub with gardening gloves on. You *appreciate* the effort, but you can't help thinking:

This is just more work for me.

THE SCROLL AND SIGH

I tried meditation for a while. Trying to keep that sacred 'me time' was like wrestling a crocodile—the jaws of obligation snapping shut about 30 minutes before I was due to leave.

'But I have this to do … and that to prepare … and I think I'm late on the credit card.'

Then I'd come up for air and try to rationalise it. It's just 60 minutes. The house won't burn down. (Maybe)

The meditation teacher, of course, was always Zen—like a requirement of the role. When she suggested I 'carve out nourishing space' each day,

This Wasn't the Plam

I nearly snorted. Turns out it's a lot easier to find nourishing space when you live alone and only work part-time doing sound baths.

I wanted to hand her a schedule of my week and ask which nourishing pocket she'd like to crawl into. Or better—invite her over for a one-week life swap.

But here's the kicker: She wasn't wrong.

I didn't have to be the one doing the laundry, organising the dental appointments, or picking up the scattered life admin that everyone else 'forgot'. I could've waited until someone ran out of socks. Could've let it all drop.

But I didn't. I just didn't have the strength to let the chaos unfold.

If I'm being even more honest, I think I was terrified.

Because if I wasn't the one managing it all, who would I be?

THE REALISATION / GRIEF OF LOSING THE ROLE

No one tells you that when your kids grow up and start needing you less, it doesn't feel like liberation.

It feels like being quietly written out of a story you spent decades writing.

You nod, you smile—*'Go, sweetheart, go live your life'*—and somewhere behind your ribcage, the ache of redundancy settles in.

I had spent so long stitching my worth into every packed lunch, every late-night pickup, every solved crisis. I thought when the need faded, freedom would flood in.

Instead, there was only silence. And questions.

What was I building toward if it wasn't this?

What dreams did I archive while folding other people's futures into shape?

Space arrived, but it didn't feel like an opportunity.

It felt like walking into a house I owned but never truly moved into.

And somewhere in that hollow quiet, a new question began to rise—not about what I had lost, but about what might still be waiting for me.

ENLIGHTENMENT ENVY

Those 'freedom mums' whose kids had actually flown the coop—they looked so ... free.

Photos of solo wine tastings, mothers and daughters with perfect makeup, yoga poses on cliffs.

I admired them. Sort of.

But I also wondered if they were missing out.

This Wasn't the Plan

They weren't in the Peace Room for the chats. They weren't baking for Granpa. They weren't still here—exhausted and loved and occasionally hiding from their family in the pantry with a KitKat.

Maybe their lives looked better.

But mine still felt full. Even if it came with a side of rage and mouldy towels.

LUXURY ON A LOOP

Freedom wasn't just far away. It felt like it was orbiting Mars.

Every time I thought I was close, another responsibility stepped up.

Son moving back home. Granpa giving up driving (necessary but chaotic). COVID. Market crashes. The whole buffet of life interruptions.

Did we travel? Yes.

But the whole time I was gone, I carried a rock of worry in my stomach.

What if something happened? What if I missed a crisis?

What if the whole thing fell apart without me?

Mel Robinson

THE PRICE OF FREEDOM

You want to know the cost of freedom?

Try doing laundry for 30 years and then having someone say, 'Why don't you take a break? You deserve it.'

Too late, sweetheart. That ship didn't just sail—it sank with all my socks and self-worth on board.

Could I have spent that time differently?

Of course.

Would I have?

I honestly don't know.

COMPARING LIVES, LOSING MYSELF

There were days I didn't even know what I wanted.

I'd spent so long measuring my days against other people's highlight reels that I forgot what my own dreams even looked like.

Who am I when I'm not being helpful?

It's a question I'm still answering. Slowly. With more silence. More honesty. More coffee.

And less laundry.

WHAT GOES AROUND ...

Funny thing—my daughter now understands what I carried.

Not because I told her.

Because she lived it.

She's there now—shouldering the load, feeling the invisible weight.

And for once, I didn't need to explain how exhausting it all was. She'd seen it. Lived it. Said it out loud—back in the Peace Room, when she finally understood.

That mattered.

It didn't fix everything. But it made the ache a little softer.

Mel Robinson

REFLECTION

I used to believe freedom would arrive like a champagne pop—sudden, fizzy, obvious.

It didn't.

It arrived quietly. Unevenly. Wrapped in grief, and guilt, and the sound of the boyfriend doing dishes without being asked.

And yes, sometimes I still scroll past someone's Santorini sunrise post and feel like freedom is a story someone else got to live.

But now, I say this instead:

Maybe it wasn't a lie. Maybe it just wasn't my chapter ... yet.

And when my chapter comes?

You'll find me journaling on a plane.

Heading somewhere that smells like saffron, sea air, and finally—finally—*me*.

CHAPTER 7:
Turns Out, I Was Always the Main Character

WHEN I STOPPED SAYING 'YES' AUTOMATICALLY

It crept in quietly—the first time I said 'no', not because I had a clash in the calendar, but because I simply didn't want to.

Not my circus. Not my monkey. Not my turn to be emotionally available for everyone else's drama.

And to my great surprise?

The world didn't end.

No one fainted.

The group chat moved on without me—and I exhaled for the first time in months.

I used to think that being available made me valuable. But it turns out peace tastes better than praise.

LITTLE ACTS OF REBELLION (THAT FELT LIKE LIBERATION)

There's a kind of freedom that lives in small moments.

Lighting a candle. Taking a bath.

Buying the 'good cheese' and *not sharing it*.

Eating it in silence, on the couch, with no shame and an old rom-com.

Liberation.

And yes—maybe I did book a retreat and only told the family once I'd packed the car.

'I'll be back Friday,' I said, driving off like some middle-aged outlaw with a boot full of protein bars and incense.

These little rebellions? They're sacred now. Not because they're dramatic. But because they're mine.

THE TRIP (REAL OR IMAGINED)

Turning 50 was looming, and everyone around me was planning parties and photo booths.

Me? I wanted a hotel room and a 'Do Not

This Wasn't the Plan

Disturb' sign.

But then I remembered the Camino—a journey I'd once dreamt about in a sleep-deprived haze years ago. The 800+ km version sounded like punishment, but the short one? 120 km. With actual beds. And meals. And maybe a bit of spiritual healing on the side? Now we're talking.

It was perfect.

No one wanted to come with me—tick.

Didn't require matching napkins—tick.

And I could finally use my passport for something other than family emergencies—tick.

There were nerves, of course. I'd never travelled overseas solo. My support crew was on the other side of the planet, and if I broke down mid-walk, I wasn't sure who'd come. But I went.

And just before I left, Mum gave me a hug, tear in her eye, and said, 'I always wanted to do that walk … but we left it too late.'

Cue emotional violins. So, I walked for both of us.

And here's the kicker:

The kitchen survived.

There were no hospital trips.

No meltdowns.

No messages from the brink.

They didn't need me.

And that felt … strange.
But also a bit magic.

INTERLUDE: RAISING EVERYONE BUT ME

No one tells you that when the needing ends, it doesn't feel like a grand finale.

It feels like slipping out the side door of a life you meticulously hosted, catered, and cleaned up after.

I smiled and said, *'Go live your life, sweetheart,'* while feeling like I was quietly misplacing my own.

At eighteen, I thought freedom was easy. I left home assuming my parents must have been desperate to get their lives back.

I didn't realise the unspoken truth: freedom, at first, feels a lot like loss.

I stayed draped in the invisible cloak of caregiving for years longer than necessary, not because they asked—but because I didn't know who I was without it.

But here's what I know now:
I am not simply useful.
I am whole.
And the space they left behind
It isn't an ending.
It's an open door back to myself.

IDENTITY SHIFTS

One day, I declared I believed in unicorns.

It started as a joke. But then … sparkly unicorn pens showed up in my handbag, and I found myself waving one in a boardroom. That was it—the official rebirth.

People didn't quite know what to do with me. But honestly? That was part of the fun.

I used to say I was the glue holding everything together.

Now I say I'm the glitter.

They'll be finding bits of me everywhere long after I'm gone.

MIDLIFE, BUT MAKE IT MAIN STAGE

These days, people look at me differently. My kids. Friends. Even myself.

There's a softness that's replaced the martyrdom. A calm that feels earned.

If I could write a letter to my younger self, it would say:

> *You think this pace, this burnout, this invisible grind is the price of a good life. But what's ahead is not a void. It's peace.*

Mel Robinson

*It's the chance to become the version of yourself that's not just useful—but whole.
So hang in there, wild-hearted wonder woman.
You're not fading.
You're forging.*

This Wasn't the Plam

FREEDOM IN THE MUNDANE

I think back to the time when the kids were young but noticeably growing up. It was the first time I remembered eating hot food at a restaurant *without interruption*. No tiny voice asking for ketchup. No reheating.

Actual warm food.
It was divine.
And I cried a little. Because I realised …
This was the dream.
Freedom doesn't always look like Italy.
Sometimes, it's just eating your damn meal while it's hot.

THE GIFT OF NOT BEING NEEDED (ALL THE TIME)

Have the kids stepped back?
Sort of.
Like slow astronauts detaching from the mothership—awkwardly and with lots of emotional radio static.
And in that quiet? I panicked.
Then I sorted drawers.
Then I sat still.
And now? I'm learning.

To nap without guilt.
To walk just because.
To let the silence sit beside me and not fill it with usefulness.
I used to believe being indispensable was my superpower.
Turns out, being at peace? Is even better.

REFLECTION

So where does that leave me now?
Still a mum. Still a daughter. Still human.
But also …
A woman with a passport.
A unicorn pen.
And a growing suspicion that *this*—this peace, this quiet certainty—was what I was chasing all along.
The freedom I was promised used to feel like a story someone else got to live.
Maybe it wasn't a lie.
Maybe it just wasn't my chapter … until now.
And now that I'm finally the main character?
Well, let's just say …
I've got plans.

CHAPTER 8:
It's Fine ... Until It Isn't

THE PARTY, THE PENDANT, AND THE PLASTIC PLANTS

We had finally done it.
A real holiday. No kids. No emergencies. Just the two of us, a packed bag, and a calendar that wasn't colour-coded with other people's needs. I even remember thinking—we made it. This was the reward. The adulting finish line. I was almost smug.

I'd asked Mum to water the houseplants while we were away. The kids were home, but let's be honest—if I'd left it to them, I'd have returned to a kitchen that looked like the final scene of a post-apocalyptic zombie film, with a few half-dead succulents barely hanging on for dear life. Mum, of course, said yes. She always said yes. And she loved those kinds of little jobs—being useful, helpful, present.

When we got back, the house did look like a brothel-cyclone hybrid. There was a weird smell, an ungodly number of dirty mugs in the lounge, and something unidentifiable growing in the bathroom. But my plants? Glorious. Vibrant. Alive. Mum had done her job to an A+ standard.

It wasn't until a bit later that I noticed the watermarks. I was dusting the mantle—yes, dusting, a rare and noble act—and I saw a suspicious puddle under one of the little faux potted plants. I leaned in. Water. I checked the next one. Also wet. Slowly it dawned on me: she'd watered the plastic plants, too.

And that was Mum in a nutshell. Loyal. Dutiful. Doting. Doing the job, whether it made sense or not. She didn't question—she just cared.

We all laughed about it. At the time.

But now? It's one of those memories that sits in my chest like a stone.

Because not long after that … the end began.

This Wasn't the Plam

BEFORE I HAD THE WORDS

There's no ceremony when the end begins.

No line in the sand. No email with a subject line: *It's happening now, FYI*. Just a slow shift. The kind you feel in your gut long before your brain lets you name it.

Mum had been fading for a while. Not in a dramatic, tragic movie-scene way. It was smaller than that. Quieter. Missed appointments. Forgotten pin numbers. A walk to the shops that turned into a search party.

I remember the moment that gut-punch hit— when she missed the dentist appointment because she forgot why she'd even gone into town.

THE MOMENT THAT SHOOK ME

Living close to the CBD meant Mum and Dad could jump on the local bus for appointments, errands— sometimes just to argue over superannuation and milkshakes.

It was oddly romantic, the kind of quiet partnership you admire … until it starts to fray.

This day was different.

Mum had a solo dentist appointment—easy enough. She knew the route. She knew the bus stop.

But she didn't show up.

The dentist called:

'Is your mum okay? She missed her appointment.'

Panic bloomed.

No answer on Mum's phone. Dad fumbling with his mobile. Time ticking.

An hour passed. Then another.

We debated calling the police, the hospital, canvassing the streets.

Finally, the phone rang.

It was Mum. Cheerful.

'Why all the fuss? I'm fine. I'm just in the gardens.'

The gardens were half a kilometre from the dentist.

'Mum,' I asked carefully, 'do you remember why you're in town?'

Silence.

'No … What was on today?'

That was the moment.

Not funny, not fixable.

Not like the time she made a cake with cornflour instead of icing sugar and tried to kill us all with gags and giggles.

This was different.

This was the gut punch.

It wasn't funny anymore. It wasn't even just concerning. It was terrifying.

We danced around the word for a while. *Dementia.* It sounds so clinical. So final. But it was there, like a shadow on the wall. No matter how brightly we kept the lights on, it loomed.

Dad did what dads do—he soldiered on.

And my coping mechanism, as always, was to make a plan:

The emergency watch. The location-tracking phone. The medicine schedules.

I became nurse, organiser, coach, translator, daughter.

All at once.

There was still a lot of love. But it came layered with dread. Like a meal you know will make you sick, but you eat it anyway because it's your favourite.

That's what caring for her became—something I loved that slowly undid me.

THE SLOW FADE

After that day, 'It's fine' became Mum's catchphrase—and my quiet alarm bell.

The forgetting gathered momentum.

Appointments. PINs. Names.

The computer she once ruled like a kingdom turned into an unsolvable maze.

Dad stepped in—bills, meds, passwords.

But it was clear he was trying to hold back the tide with a teaspoon.

There was no dramatic moment.

No diagnosis wrapped in a bow.

Just a slow, stubborn erosion.

And me, filling the cracks with effort.

Like I could outrun it if I worked hard enough.

THE GRIEF SPIRAL

Grief doesn't always wait for death.

Sometimes, it shows up in small ways—like watching your mum struggle to log into the bank account she once balanced better than any budget spreadsheet on earth. Or watching her stare blankly at her own birthday card, not quite sure what the inside joke meant anymore.

I kept showing up. Checking her medications. Monitoring meals. Answering questions kindly, even when it was the third time that day.

Meanwhile, the kids were spiralling through Uni assignments and job anxiety and boyfriend dramas. There was no 'easy' wing of this house anymore.

It wasn't just multitasking.

This Wasn't the Plam

It was caregiving on both ends—young adults still learning how to fly, and elderly parents quietly forgetting how to walk.

THE COLD REALISATION

We built the granny flat—Granma's Cubby—so Mum and Dad could stay independent, close by, dignified.

It was a good plan. Noble, even.

But reality doesn't honour blueprints.

Staying close meant being the tech support.

The emergency contact.

The quiet lifeline woven into every day.

And somewhere along the way, without a ceremony or a title change, I stopped being just a daughter.

I became the safety net.

The unspoken Plan B.

The person who would always know what to do next.

That was never the plan.

But plans are for people who get to choose.

Mel Robinson

THE CROSS OF CARE

No one tells you when it happens. There's no announcement.

No blinking red light.

You just notice something off—and step in.

Then again.

And again.

Until one day, you realise you're living on high alert:

Softening every blow for aging parents who don't want to admit they're slipping.

Shielding young adults still learning how to fall and get back up.

Managing yourself with a level of silence that should probably be a crime.

Home didn't feel like home anymore.

It felt like a triage unit where no one even remembered you were supposed to be a person too.

THE BREAKDOWN THAT DIDN'T HAPPEN

I fantasised about running away.

Not in a dramatic way—more like a midlife teenage rebellion.

What if I just drove to the beach and disappeared for 48 hours?

What if no one could find me?

Would the house implode? Would anyone even *try* to wash a dish?

But I never packed the bag. Because I knew what would happen if I left:

Mum would start trying to cook again.

Dad would attempt to fill the void and likely electrocute himself on the kettle.

The kids would try to help, but end up needing more help.

The fridge would run out of milk, and someone would cry about it.

I didn't run.

I stayed.

And the worst part? I stopped even resenting it.

THE LINES I NEVER SAID (BUT WANTED TO)

- 'Why did I agree to live with my parents for my entire adult life?'
- 'Why can't I have the life my kids do?'
- 'Could someone—anyone—look after me for a day?'

But I didn't say them.

Because I was too busy refilling prescriptions and topping up the internet data and making sure there was soy milk in the fridge.

Mel Robinson

THE WORDS I NEEDED TO HEAR

Maybe I didn't believe every word yet.

Maybe I still woke up ready to triage everyone else's emergencies before my own feet even hit the floor.

Maybe I still answered text messages like I was on call for emotional dispatch.

But here's what I remembered:

I am not the backup plan for everyone else's life.

I am not the safety net, the nurse, the unpaid emotional concierge.

I am the headline, not the footnote.

And I don't owe anyone my burnout as proof of my love.

If life was going to keep handing me broken pieces to fix, fine.

I'd start by gluing myself back together first.

CHAPTER 9:
The Hospital Visit That Wasn't

SAYING GOODBYE, SORT OF

It started like it always did: a cough, a chest infection, a hospital trip.

I'd caught a charming lurgy on the plane home—sounded like I'd taken up a pack-a-day habit just for fun—and the hospital said no visiting. Infection control.

I didn't push. It was always the same cycle: antibiotics, a bit of a grumble about the food, then back home.

Except this time, it wasn't.

We had a meeting with the doctor at 1 pm.

By 4 pm, she was gone.

There was technically time to say goodbye. But not enough to feel like it counted.

I still don't know if she knew I was there. Maybe that's a mercy. Maybe that's the kind of wound that never quite scabs over.

GRIEF, IN TRIPLICATE

Grief would've been easier with a pause button. But instead, it came with:
- Catering orders
- Editable PDFs
- Death notices
- Trying to explain digital passwords to Dad
- Making phone calls no one wants to make

Mum didn't want a funeral. She wanted a party. So, we gave her one.

Bright colours. Her artwork on display. Walls of family photos. Enough food to feed a wedding. And no alcohol—her only firm request.

It was beautiful. And surreal. Like a retirement party where the guest of honour left early and forgot to give a speech.

Dad buried his grief in logistics—legal docs, insurance policies, superannuation balances, and warranties for toasters that hadn't worked in a decade.

I buried mine under platters of sandwiches and emergency tissues.

THE DAUGHTER WHO COULDN'T SPEAK

My daughter was hit hardest.

She and Mum had their own secret language—silly words, shared jokes, quiet rituals no one else was ever invited into.

She didn't tell work. She didn't want sympathy. She just … folded in.

And I watched it happen, while trying to hold everyone else up.

THE RING THAT VANISHED

Mum's engagement ring was meant to come to me. In the will.

Just like she'd passed down her own mother's ring when I got married.

It was our tradition. A matriarchal legacy. A symbol of strong hands passed down.

But a year before she died, it went missing.

We searched everywhere—drawers, jewellery boxes, pockets, tins. Nothing.

Same with the pendant I wore on my wedding

day. 'Something old.' Something hers.

Gone.

I think the dementia stole them. Or maybe she hid them too well. Maybe they're still tucked away, waiting to be found in a coat pocket when I'm eighty.

But it wasn't just the objects that went missing. It was the plan. The story I'd imagined passing on.

A love story, interrupted.

WHAT SHE MISSED

Six months later, both kids bought their first homes.

She would've *loved* that.

All those years of saving. The heartbreak of trying. The open homes. The real estate lies. The Goldilocks properties that were always just out of reach.

And then—finally—it happened.

Granpa was glowing. But his eyes were wet. Not just with joy, but with grief.

That milestone—*the* milestone—came without her.

And that, I think, is what grief really is.

Not just the missing. Not even the memories. It's the *almosts*.

The 'she would've loved this' moments that

sneak up on you like a sad song on shuffle.

THE WALK SHE NEVER TOOK

In her final weeks, I was talking to Mum on the phone in the hospital, and she asked how the Camino was. Although I had returned from Spain, the Camino trip was six years ago. She told me she always wanted to walk the Camino, which she had told me six years before.

She said it casually, like it was a thought that had just popped into her head. But I could hear the wistful longing behind it.

She didn't get to go.

But I did.

At the time, I put two shells on my backpack, declaring Mum and Dad for all to see, feeling like they were there with me every step. Through the ache, the sweat, the mornings when I questioned my sanity. Through the golden light and donkey crossings and quiet chapels.

When I got my pilgrim stamp, I imagined slipping it into her hand and saying:

'You made it.'

Because she did.

Just not in the way we expected.

Mel Robinson

GRANPA WATCH AND ROLE REVERSALS

My daughter—baker, meal prep queen—keeps Granpa stocked with cakes and frozen meals labelled in neat handwriting like it's a food truck for seniors.

Even the boyfriend (quiet, fridge-raiding, towel-using ninja that he is) took time off work to drive Granpa to a hospital appointment. They barely spoke. I imagine it was like a silent film—two introverts and one medical form.

And my son? He lives nearby. Pops in when he can. Not always, but when it happens, I don't have to ask.

And even though I didn't *expect* this, there's a part of me that feels guilty for letting them see this side of aging—of obligation. I never knew my grandparents in decline. Mine were mostly gone by the time I reached adult memory.

I don't want this burden to be their inheritance. But I'm also glad I'm not carrying it entirely alone anymore.

This Wasn't the Plam

REFLECTION

I thought I'd feel untethered when she died.

But instead, I felt heavier. Like the next link in the chain. The one who holds the stories. The recipes. The traditions. The grief.

All of it.

But even in her absence, she gave me one last gift:

Permission.

To go.

To live.

To stop waiting for the perfect time to be myself.

Because this life?

It's not a rehearsal.

And I don't want to save all my best stories for someone else's scrapbook.

CHAPTER 10:
The Quiet Kind of Power

THE THINGS YOU'VE LET GO

There are a few things that used to bother me. Dirty uniforms. Stinky towels. Let me explain.

My daughter worked at KFC during high school. She was a good worker—the kind who'd get called in when someone else bailed on a shift. But KFC only handed out two uniforms to part-timers, and after a night surrounded by oil, batter, and mystery gravy, you didn't just smell like chicken—you became chicken.

Being the devoted mother I was, I soaked those uniforms like I was prepping them for sainthood. Nappy San. Pino Clean. Hung in the sun like sacrificial offerings. I took it personally—if she rocked up smelling like a deep fryer, what would people think of me?

Until one day, as I was dry-heaving in the laundry over a gravy-scented polo, I stopped mid-gag and realised no one cared. No one was sniffing her collar and writing up parenting reports. My daughter shrugged, said she smelled like everyone else, and that was that.

Why was I fighting so hard for clean uniforms no one cared about? It wasn't hygiene. It was pride. It was performative parenting. And in that moment, I quietly resigned from the role of Stain Removal Vigilante.

Updated quote:

'I used to be the fragrance police. Now I let them marinate in their own consequences.'

THE NEW COMPASS

My new compass doesn't point toward the laundry.

If someone leaves a wet towel to rot in the bathroom? I've got my own, thanks. If someone runs out of clean clothes? Smells like a 'them' problem.

When did this glorious shift happen? Somewhere between 'just helping out' and 'scheduling your dentist appointments while stirring dinner and booking Dad's eye surgery'.

This phase? It belongs to me. And I don't mean that metaphorically. I mean, get your own damn towel.

WHEN THE NOISE QUIETED

I was in the Peace Room, reading a book—and not just the first chapter, either. I was deep into it. The house was silent. The kind of silence that used to make me suspicious, like someone had left the front door open or climbed the pantry shelves looking for Nutella.

But this time? It was just ... quiet.

And suddenly, I froze. What do I do with this? Should I journal about it? Light a candle? Post on socials?

It was like bumping into the ghost of my mother whispering, '*This is the peace I asked for.*' And I didn't know whether to cry, panic, or grab another chapter. That silence, though? It wasn't absence.

It was an invitation.

BEING SEEN DIFFERENTLY

As the kids finally flew the coop (for real this time), something odd happened—space opened up. Not just in the wardrobe (though, yes, I can see between coat hangers now), but in my days. In my mind.

I cleaned. I rearranged paintings. I decluttered five years of expired flours I was keeping for no reason except that someone might bake again one day. And when the day's clearing was done, I didn't jump straight into dinner prep. I flopped onto the couch and said, 'I'm exhausted—let's go out.'

And no one argued.

This isn't about 'getting my life back'. It's about finally stepping into the one I'd been deferring.

CALLBACK:

I used to say, 'I'm just Mum.'
Now I say, 'I'm still Mum. And so much more.'

Mel Robinson

THE EMOTION HANGOVER

Once a month, I meet a friend at the local markets. We pretend it's about fresh veggies, but it's really our joint therapy session. One particular Saturday, it all came out. Rage. Grief. A sob-fest that would make Oprah hand over a tissue.

My friend didn't flinch. She nodded, patted my arm, and let the emotional flood spill across the market bench.

Afterward, I was mortified. Had I just ugly cried about my family in public? What if she judged me? What if she slowly ghosted me for being too raw, too messy?

But she didn't. She sent a check-in text. Met me again the next week. And I realised I'd been storing grief in my bones like a hoarder in a reality show. No wonder I was tired.

LETTER TO MY FIVE-YEARS-AGO SELF:

Thank you for holding it all.
But you don't have to anymore.

This Wasn't the Plam

THE THREADS THAT REMAIN

The family dinners stayed. That's one thread I'll keep.

Everyone gathers once a week—me, the kids, Granpa, plus whatever friend or stray partner is orbiting the family unit. The food is homemade (usually by me), the banter is ridiculous, and it's one of the few times we all sit still long enough to see each other.

That rhythm matters. Not out of obligation, but because it holds us together. Not everything old is worth keeping. But some threads? Some threads are gold.

Cue: I'm no longer the default.
But I'm still the anchor.

WISDOM, SASS, OR BOTH?

What do I say now that shocks my younger self?
I don't owe anyone a damn explanation.
Twenty-something me would have typed a three-paragraph apology for breathing too loudly. But me now? Boundary queen. If it doesn't feel right, I'm not going. If it's not my circus, I'm not stepping in the tent.

Best wisdom I've earned?

If they're offended by your boundary, they were benefiting from your lack of one.

Let that one marinate in your inbox. People-pleasing was just fear in lipstick. And I'm not doing full-face makeup for emotional freeloaders anymore.

Tattoo for my metaphorical biceps?

Return to sender.

Every guilt trip. Every passive-aggressive task. Every 'But we were counting on you.'

Stamp it. Send it back.

ZINGER MEDLEY:

- 'You can't guilt-trip someone who's unsubscribed from the newsletter.'
- 'I didn't disappear. I just stopped narrating everyone else's story.'
- 'I'm not cold. I'm healed. There's a difference.'

REFLECTION

Is this peace?

Maybe. But it feels deeper than that.

It's the absence of chasing. The exhale after years of holding your breath. The soft sound of your own thoughts … without interruption.

It's not fireworks. It's a warm cup of tea you

actually get to finish.

It's mine.

And I don't have to shrink to fit into it anymore.

WHO AM I NOW?

I'm not the family planner, the snack fairy, the calendar keeper.

I'm the woman who finally gets to say, 'Not today.'

I'm still healing. Still showing up. But now, I'm showing up for me, too.

And if I'm the main character now?

It's not because I demanded it.

It's because I finally stopped casting myself as support.

CLOSER:

I thought I'd have to fight for this chapter. But it turns out, it waited patiently for me all along.

CHAPTER 11:
The Great Australian Lie: Owning a Home Without a Miracle

THE HOME OWNERSHIP DREAM

Buying a house used to be a badge of adulthood. First, you bought a car (preferably not one that doubled as a rust farm), then you scrimped and saved and bought a house. You were *in*. You'd arrived.

My husband and I tried to pass down the wisdom of the 'starter home'. We explained—often, and with increasingly dramatic hand gestures—that your first property would not be your forever dream home. Ours certainly wasn't. It was the ugliest house on the street … which, funnily enough, funded our future dream house.

We tried to gently rebrand adulthood for the kids: not something shiny, but something earned.

Our eldest—determined, driven, and very good at spotting parental weaknesses—secured a sweet deal early on. Her dad agreed to match whatever she saved for her first car. So she lived like a monk. By the time she was test-driving vehicles, she had thousands saved … and her eye on a *new* car.

We grumbled. We groaned. But we were secretly proud.

So when the house-buying conversations began, we braced.

THE FINANCIAL REALITY

The market was ridiculous. Properties vanished faster than toilet paper in a pandemic. Auction reserves were a fantasy. Open homes looked like mini music festivals.

We had the conversations about deposits, stamp duty (which my daughter correctly identified as a government scam), and whether we could 'help out' if the perfect place came along.

Mel Robinson

I refused to agree to anything without legal representation present.

We started the inspection trail. For *three years*. Every Saturday. A list of options in hand. Each one dismissed for being:

- Too small
- Too far
- Too ugly
- Too damp
- Too murdery

We entered what I now call the **Goldilocks Phase of Property Hunting**.

And still, she saved. Relentlessly. No rent. No lifestyle inflation. Just a quiet determination … and an increasing sense that this was all going to fall back on us.

This Wasn't the Plam

DELAYED DREAMS

Every year we hoped the market would calm. Every year it got worse.

There was a moment—maybe eighteen months in—where we all just … gave up a bit. The realisation dawned that, unless a miracle dropped from the sky, this might be the plan. Forever.

Granma, sadly, didn't live to see either child buy a house. That fact sits in me like a stone.

Because not long after she passed—within six months, in fact—**both kids bought houses**. Within weeks of each other. A double shock.

They weren't their dream homes. But they were proud. Determined. And ready.

Granpa was overjoyed. Quietly heartbroken that Granma missed it. But bursting with pride all the same.

THE EMOTIONAL COST

We tried to support them emotionally more than financially. But there were plenty of tight moments—implied asks, near misses, the occasional plea for a 'short-term float'.

I kept thinking:

This wasn't meant to be my job. Did I sign up to

carry them into middle age?

And then the quieter truth:

They're trying. Really trying. But everything is stacked against them.

It was the hardest kind of support—watching them build something with every tool *except* the privilege you were raised with.

GENERATIONAL DIVIDE

We had it hard too—sure. Interest rates at 17%. No tech jobs. No parental bail-outs.

But back then, housing wasn't *impossible*. It was hard, not soul-crushing. There weren't 200 people lining up at every open home. There weren't pre-approval lotteries and vendors who vanished like ghosts.

This generation didn't grow up lazy. They grew up priced out.

And still, they're trying.

And that's what I'll remember

Not the whinging.

Not the fights.

Not the real estate agents with the emotional range of a potato.

Just that they kept showing up.

This Wasn't the Plam

ZINGERS, QUOTES AND REAL LINES

- 'It's only $50K. It's not like I'm asking for a kidney.'
- 'You're nearly retired—you must be loaded.'
- 'We'll totally pay you back.'
- 'This place doesn't flood.' (Mum opens the flood map to find Noah's ark floating past.)

And my personal favourite:

- 'It was so much easier in your day.'

Right. Yes. I'm *old*, therefore *rich*. Classic boomer logic ... except I'm not a boomer. I'm a tired Gen Xer with aging parents, a slow-draining super account, and one working knee.

Mel Robinson

REFLECTION

They bought homes. Finally. It happened.

And as I watched them hold their keys for the first time, something shifted in me.

Yes, there was pride. Of course there was. But also grief. That Granma didn't see it. That it took so long. That 'buying a house' had become the Everest of their twenties.

It shouldn't have been this hard. And yet, here we are.

The miracle didn't drop from the sky.

They built it.

With grit.

And, probably, just a little help from Mum and Dad.

CHAPTER 12:
The New Juggle

LIFE NOW?

Well, both kids are out of the house (hallelujah), but the emotional group chat still pings like it's a full-time job.

We host family dinner every week. Mandatory. No excuses. Granpa comes too, and we all gather around the table for a chaotic symphony of updates: workplace drama, relationship gossip, real estate commentary, existential dread, and unsolicited political takes.

Dinner is mainly cooked by me. Leftovers are taken by them. And it all just ... works.

Most of the time.

ZINGERS YOU MIGHT DROP NOW

- 'Yes, thank you for realising my life was not a luxury resort.'
- 'Turns out emotional labour doesn't count as cardio—or a retirement plan.'
- 'I don't need a medal. Just maybe someone else to load the dishwasher.'

TEXT EXCHANGE ON FAMILY CHAT:

Me: 'Family dinner at 6:30 pm Wednesday.'
Daughter: 'Will there be dessert?'
Son: 'Can I bring a plus one?'
Daughter again: 'Can you make extra so I've got lunch for Thursday?'

Kill me now. But also, don't.
Because I love them.
But still. Kill me. *A little bit.*

REFLECTION

Things are shifting. Slowly. Imperfectly. But undeniably.

They're starting to see me—not just as the emotional vending machine who dispenses love and lasagne—but as a woman. A human. One who gets tired. One who *was always tired*.

And does it help, being seen?

Yes.

But it also sharpens the ache of how long I wasn't.

If I could go back to my mid-crisis self, whisper something into her exhausted brain, I'd say,

It's going to feel like everything matters. It doesn't. Breathe anyway.

That panic spiral? Temporary.

The fear of never being free? Fuzzy now.

That moment you thought you were failing? Turns out, you were *moulting*.

You're not behind. You're in transition. Becoming someone who can hold more than she thought possible. Someone who finally understands that silence, boredom, and chaos are all part of becoming.

And to that inner crisis goblin still yelling in your chest?

You're not lost.
You're just not there yet.
But you will be.

CHAPTER 13:
This Was Never Just About Them

THE GRIEF HAS STOPPED SCREAMING AND STARTED TO WHISPER.

LOOKING BACKWARD, LOOKING INWARD

Ten years ago, I would never have imagined myself in this position.

I knew my parents wouldn't live forever, but you never really imagine them ... *gone*. And yes, the plan was always for the kids to grow up and go, but I don't think I understood what that would actually feel like. Not really. The fantasies I had? They were more like movie scenes I'd borrowed.

This Wasn't the Plam

Nothing real. Nothing mine.

Maybe I didn't let the fantasy go too far—just in case it didn't happen and I'd be disappointed.

But if I could look at my life now through the eyes of that version of me, ten years younger and already running on empty, I think she'd smirk with a quiet pride.

Two fiercely independent kids, holding their own in the world. Paying bills. Voting. Filing taxes. Keeping Granpa company, even when it's hard. And me? Not as shattered as I feared. Not as invisible as I once felt.

It wasn't the horror story I imagined. It was just … life. Unfolding. Unfiltered. And maybe, at the time, I was too tired to dream of something this grounded, this human, this whole.

REDEFINING 'PURPOSE'

What if I never figure out what I'm here to do?

It's a thought that's haunted me for decades. I kept chasing the perfect label—the one that would feel like a soul contract. But every time I tried to define it, I drew a blank.

Possibilities felt endless. Which meant overwhelming. What if I picked wrong? What if I ruined the rest of my life?

So I kept doing what I'd always done: what was expected.

But now? With the dust a little more settled and my mum's absence echoing louder than her presence used to—I'm done handing down guilt and duty like heirlooms. I want to leave a different kind of legacy. One made of boundaries, honesty, and *soft, sacred nos*.

Let that be the inheritance.

Looking back now, the woman I was then—exhausted, multitasking, invisible in her own story—feels like someone I loved but hadn't yet forgiven. Today, I can say it: I am not just a support crew. I am not the background music. I am the main character. The mother, the daughter, the woman with dreams that deserve centre stage. This isn't the ending. It's the beginning—one I get to write, in my own ink, for the first time.

THE PEACE THAT DOESN'T NEED PROOF

This book began on a new kind of day.

Reflexology. Massage. A long lunch for a girlfriend's birthday. No guilt. No agenda. Just time because I could take it.

That's peace.

Not the inactive kind I used to scoff at—but

This Wasn't the Plan

the kind that wraps around you like your favourite jumper. A quiet comfort. A cuppa alone. A thought that doesn't spiral.

I used to think peace was boring. I was wrong.

Now, it's a holy thing.

WHAT YOU'RE WEAVING FORWARD

Some traditions I'll keep. Others I'll bend until they look like me.

Christmas used to be Mum's domain—sweating over a roast in the Queensland heat, panicking over presentation like it would hold the family together for another year. When she passed, the torch came straight to me.

But this isn't her kitchen, and I'm not chasing her perfection.

Yes, we still do the turkey—with her stuffing. But the glaze is new. The cake is vegan. The playlist is different. It's not a replication; it's a remix.

That's the real inheritance.

Same goes for the emotional load. My kids have seen what it costs to keep everyone comfortable while you dissolve inside. And they're choosing differently. Watching them reject martyrdom is, in its own way, a kind of miracle.

The Peace Room still stands. It's used now for

planning, dreaming, decompressing. One day, I imagine grandkids curled up on the couch asking for the story of how their parents bought their first house. I'll tell it with love—and a healthy side of sarcasm.

We'll call it *intergenerational therapy*.

THE NEW SHAPE OF SELF
WHO AM I NOW, WITH NO ONE ELSE TO PERFORM FOR?

Honestly?

I'm a damn relief.

To myself, mostly.

I'm not dressing for approval. I'm not curating my opinions to make everyone else feel safe. I'm not holding back the eye roll or the joy or the deep, unruly laugh that used to make me feel 'too much'.

And is this who I imagined I'd become?

Not even close.

She's better.

She's softer, louder, quieter, stronger. Less performative. More true.

And the most 'me' thing I've done lately?

This Wasn't the Plam

WRITING THIS BOOK.

A memoir soaked in truth, sass, grief, glitter, and resistance. A story that doesn't apologise. That says the quiet parts out loud and dares you to look away.
This book is not just a record.
It's a reclamation.
Of space. Of voice. Of self.

FINAL LETTER TO THE READER
DEAR READER,

If you've made it this far, first of all — congratulations. You've survived the emotional obstacle course that is my life story: complete with maternal devotion, burnt-out dreams, identity meltdowns, and the slow, delicious unfurling of a woman who finally realised she was never meant to be everyone's backbone and nobody's priority.

You've witnessed the tightrope walk between love and loss, guilt and grace. You've seen me rage in the Peace Room, rewrite résumés while crying into tea, and gently, painfully, outgrow a version of myself that kept everyone fed, organised, healed … except me.

Mel Robinson

BUT LET'S BE CLEAR: THIS WASN'T A STORY ABOUT SACRIFICE.

This was a resurrection.

And if something in these pages has made you uncomfortable, reflective, or wildly inspired to throw someone's emotional baggage back into their lap—then excellent. That means something here landed.

You might be reading this in your thirties, forties, fifties, sixties—hell, maybe you're a secret emotional prodigy in your twenties (doubtful, but we'll humour the idea).

Maybe you're in the thick of child rearing, or freshly unhooked from the identity of 'Mum' and wondering who this quieter version of you is.

Or maybe you're the daughter. Or the son. Or the partner. Reading this with a quiet dawning realisation that your mother, or someone like her, may have been doing all of this under your nose—gracefully, invisibly, and sometimes resentfully. Maybe you're just now starting to see her not as a fixture, but as a person.

Good. Keep looking.

This book is not here to wrap things up in a bow. It's here to hand you the ribbon and say: **Go tie your own damn life together—on your terms**.

This Wasn't the Plam

You might be burnt out, bruised, or barely hanging on. But here's the good news:
You're also still here.
And you?
You are not too late.
You are not too old.
You are not too broken.
And you are not selfish for wanting more.
The version of you who was always 'fine'?
She deserves rest.
And boundaries.
And joy without apology.
So here's my parting advice, from one recovering over-functioner to another:
Wear the outfit.
Speak the truth.
Say no without writing a novella.
Stop editing your joy to make other people more comfortable.
And never again shrink just to fit inside someone else's expectations.
Because, darling?
The real you takes up space.
And we are all better for it.
With love,
Reluctant Queen of Unpaid Emotional Labour

Mel Robinson

(formerly known as Mum / Daughter / Employee / She Who Carries It All)

P.S. Burn the martyr cape. Keep the crown and glitter.

A NOTE FROM THE AUTHOR

If you enjoyed this book, I would be very grateful if you could write a review and publish it at your point of purchase. Your review, even a brief one, will help other readers to decide whether they'll enjoy my work.

If you want to be notified of new releases from myself and other Alkira Publishing authors, please **sign up to the Alkira Publishing email list**. In return you'll get a free ebook by an Alkira Publishing author. You'll find the sign-up button on the right-hand side under the photo at www.alkirapublishing.com. Of course, your information will never be shared, and the publisher won't inundate you with emails, just let you know of new releases.

www.ingramcontent.com/pod-product-compliance
Lightning Source LLC
Chambersburg PA
CBHW052213090526
44584CB00017BB/2291